Contents

THE DEATH OF REBELLION FILES

MANGAL PANDEY

MR VIVEK KUMAR PANDEY

Foreword

The Death Of Rebellion Files Is Based On True Story Of Freedom Fighter "Mangal Pandey". The Indian Rebellion of 1857 was a major uprising in India in 1857–58 against the rule of the British India.How Mangal Pandey sacrificed his life for this country. He was a hero of our country and will always be hero.During Writing This Book No Character No Religion And No Caste Are Harmed. It's Only For Study Purpose. We don't Hurt Anyone.

Preface

Author Bio

"Winner Youngest Writer Award" 1st Rank In Gujarat India.Publish 1000+ Book That Is Guinness World Record. Film Script Writer & Screen Writer. Total 60+ Own Creating LIVE Show .Nojoto Golden Mic Winner & Your Quotes Fame Star. In Age Of 14 He Publish 500+ Book. Author Fame Novel & Story Is Height Chaar Foot,Mission Kutch 1972,Pagdhal,Palsa,Radashagivri,Pushpa. He Win "Bestseller Award" & "Year Of The Entertainment" (Author). Author Say This All Credit Goes To My "Superhero" Daddy,He Always Love Me.

ONE
MANGAL PANDEY

1. Disclaimer : During writing this book no character & no religious are harmed written by Mr Vivek Kumar Pandey.

Mangal Pandey was an Indian soldier who played a key part in the events immediately preceding the outbreak of the Indian rebellion of 1857. He was a sepoy (infantryman) in the 34th Bengal Native Infantry (BNI) regiment of the British East India Company. In 1984, the Indian government issued a postage stamp to remember him. His life and actions have also been portrayed in several cinematic productions.

- Birth Place

Mangal Pandey was born in Nagwa, a village of upper Ballia district, Ceded and Conquered Provinces (now in Uttar Pradesh), to a Hindu Brahmin family. Mangal Pandey had joined the Bengal Army in 1849. In March 1857, he was a private soldier (sepoy) in the 5th Company of the 34th Bengal Native Infantry.

- Mutiny

On the afternoon of 29 March 1857, Lieutenant Baugh, Adjutant of the 34th Bengal Native Infantry, then stationed at Barrackpore was informed that several men of his regiment were in an excited state. Further, it was reported to him that one of them, Mangal Pandey, was pacing in front of the regiment's guard room by the parade ground, armed with a loaded musket, calling upon the men to rebel and threatening to shoot the first European that he set eyes on. Testimony at a subsequent enquiry recorded that Pandey, unsettled by unrest amongst the sepoys and intoxicated by the narcotic bhang, had seized his weapons and run to the quarter-guard building upon learning that a detachment of British soldiers was disembarking from a steamer near the cantonment.

Baugh immediately armed himself and galloped on his horse to the lines. Pandey took position behind the station gun, which was in front of the quarter-guard of the 34th, took aim at Baugh and fired. He missed Baugh, but the bullet struck his horse in the flank bringing both the horse and its rider down. Baugh quickly disentangled himself and, seizing one of his pistols, advanced towards Pandey and fired. He missed. Before Baugh could draw his sword, Pandey attacked him with a talwar (a heavy Indian sword) and closing with the adjutant, slashed Baugh on the shoulder and neck and brought him to the ground. It was then that another sepoy, Shaikh Paltu, intervened and tried to restrain Pandey even as he tried to reload his musket.

A British Sergeant-Major named Hewson had arrived on the parade ground, summoned by a native officer, before Baugh. He had ordered Jemadar Ishwari Prasad, the Indian officer in command of the quarter-guard, to arrest Pandey. To this, the jemadar stated that his NCOs had gone for help and that he could not take Pandey by himself. In response Hewson ordered Ishwari Prasad to fall in the guard with loaded weapons. In the meantime, Baugh had arrived on the field shouting 'Where is he? Where is he?' Hewson in reply called out to Baugh, 'Ride to the right, sir, for your life. The sepoy will fire at you!' At that point Pandey fired.

Hewson had charged towards Pandey as he was fighting with Lieutenant Baugh. While confronting Pandey, Hewson was knocked to the ground from behind by a blow from Pandey's musket. The sound of the firing had brought other sepoys from the barracks; they remained mute spectators. At this juncture, Shaikh Paltu, while trying to defend the two Englishmen called upon the other sepoys to assist him. Assailed by sepoys who threw stones and shoes at his back, Shaikh Paltu called on the guard to help him hold Pandey, but they threatened to shoot him if he did not let go of the mutineer.

Some of the sepoys of the quarter-guard then advanced and struck at the two prostrate officers. They then threatened Shaikh Paltu and ordered him to release Pandey, whom he had been vainly trying to hold back. However, Paltu continued to hold Pandey until Baugh and the sergeant-major was able to get up. Himself wounded by now, Paltu was obliged to loosen his grip. He backed away in one direction and Baugh and Hewson in another, while being struck with the butt ends of the guards' muskets.

In the meantime, a report of the incident had been carried to the commanding officer General Hearsey, who then galloped to the ground with his two officer sons. Taking in the scene, he rode up to the guard, drew his pistol and ordered them to do their duty by seizing Mangal Pandey. The General threatened to shoot the first man who disobeyed. The men of the quarter-guard fell in and followed Hearsey towards Pandey. Pandey then put the muzzle of the musket to his chest and discharged it by pressing the trigger with his foot. He collapsed bleeding, with his regimental jacket on fire, but not mortally wounded.

Pandey recovered and was brought to trial less than a week later. When asked whether he had been under the influence of any substances, he stated steadfastly that he had mutinied on his own accord and that no other person had played any part in encouraging him. He was sentenced to death by hanging, along with Jemadar Ishwari Prasad, after three Sikh members of the quarter-guard testified that the latter had ordered them not to arrest Pandey.Mangal Pandey's execution took place on 8 April. Jemadar Ishwari Prasad was executed by hanging on 21 April.

- A scene from the 1857 Indian Rebellion

The 34th B.N.I. Regiment was disbanded "with disgrace" on 6 May as a collective punishment, after an investigation by the government, for failing to perform their duty in restraining a mutinous soldier and their officer. That came after a period of six weeks while petitions for leniency were examined in Calcutta. Sepoy Shaikh Paltu was promoted to havildar (sergeant) for his behavior on 29 March but he was murdered in an isolated part of the Barrackpore cantonment shortly before the regiment was disbanded.

The Indian historian Surendra Nath Sen notes that the 34th B.N.I. had a good recent record and that the Court of Enquiry had not found any evidence of a connection with unrest at Berhampore involving the 19th B.N.I. four weeks before. However, Mangal Pandey's actions and the failure of the armed and on-duty sepoys of the quarter-guard to take action convinced the British military authorities that the whole regiment was unreliable. It appeared that Pandey had acted without first taking other sepoys into his confidence but that antipathy towards their British officers within the regiment had led most of those present to act as spectators, rather than obey orders.

· Motivation

The personal motivation behind Mangal Pandey's behaviour remains confused. During the incident itself he shouted to other sepoys: "come out – the Europeans are here"; "from biting these cartridges we shall become infidels" and "you sent me out here, why don't you follow me". At his court-martial, he stated that he had been taking bhang and opium, and was not conscious of his actions on 29 March.

There were a wide range of factors causing apprehension and mistrust in the Bengal Army immediately prior to the Barrackpore event. Pandey's reference to cartridges is usually attributed to a new type of bullet cartridge used in the Enfield P-53 rifle which was to be introduced in the Bengal Army that year. The cartridge was thought to be greased with animal fat, primarily from cows and pigs, which could not be consumed by Hindus and Muslims respectively (the former a holy animal of the Hindus and the latter being abhorrent to Muslims). The cartridges had to be bitten at one end before use. The Indian troops in some regiments were of the opinion that this was an intentional act of the British, with the aim of defiling their religions.

Colonel S. Wheeler of the 34th B.N.I. was known as a zealous Christian preacher. The wife of Captain William Halliday of the 56th B.N.I. had the Bible printed in Urdu and Hindi and distributed among the sepoys, thus raising suspicions amongst them that the British were intent on converting them to Christianity.

The 19th and 34th Bengal Native Infantry were stationed at Lucknow during the time of the annexation of Oudh in 1856 because of alleged misgovernment by the Nawab. The annexation had negative implications for sepoys in the Bengal Army (a significant portion of whom came from that princely state). Before the annexation, these sepoys had the right to petition the British Resident at Lucknow for justice — a significant privilege in the context of native courts. As a result of the East India Company's action, they lost that special status, since Oudh no longer existed as a nominally independent political entity.

The 19th B.N.I. is important because it was the regiment charged with testing the new cartridges on 26 February 1857. However, right up to the mutiny the new rifles had not been issued to them, and the cartridges in the magazine of the regiment were as free of grease as they had been through the preceding half-century. The paper used in wrapping the cartridges was of a different colour, arousing suspicions. The non-commissioned officers of the regiment refused to accept the cartridges on 26 February. This information was conveyed to the commanding officer, Colonel William Mitchell; he took it upon himself to try to convince the sepoys that the cartridges were no different from those they had been accustomed to and that they need not bite it. He concluded his exhortation with an appeal to the native officers to uphold the honour of the regiment and a threat to court-martial such sepoys as refused to accept the cartridge. However, the next morning the sepoys of the regiment seized their bell of arms (weapons store). The subsequent conciliatory behaviour of Mitchell convinced the sepoys to return to their barracks.

- Court of Enquiry

A Court of Enquiry was ordered which, after an investigation which lasted nearly a month, recommended the disbanding of the 19th B.N.I. The same was carried out on 31 March. The 19th B.N.I. were allowed to retain items of uniform and were provided by the government with allowances to return to their homes. Both Colonel Mitchell of the 19th B.N.I. and (subsequent to the incident of 29 March) Colonel Wheeler of Pandey's 34th B.N.I. were declared unsuited to take charge of any new regiments raised to replace the disbanded units.

- Consequences

The attack by and punishment of Pandey is widely seen as the opening scene of what came to be known as the Indian Rebellion of 1857. Knowledge of his action was widespread amongst his fellow sepoys and is assumed to have been one of the factors leading to the general series of mutinies that broke out during the following months. Mangal Pandey would prove to be influential for later figures in the Indian Nationalist Movement like V.D. Savarkar, who viewed his motive as one of the earliest manifestations of Indian Nationalism. Modern Indian nationalists portray Pandey as the mastermind behind a conspiracy to revolt against the British, although a recently published analysis of events immediately preceding the outbreak concludes that "there is little historical evidence to back up any of these revisionist interpretations".

During the rebellion that followed, Pandee or Pandey became the derogatory term used by British soldiers and civilians when referring to a mutinous sepoy. This was a direct derivation from the name of Mangal Pandey.

• Film, stage and literature

A film based on the sequence of events that led up to the mutiny entitled Mangal Pandey: The Rising starring Indian actor, Aamir Khan along with Rani Mukerji, Amisha Patel and Toby Stephens, directed by Ketan Mehta was released on 12 August 2005.

The life of Pandey was the subject of a stage play titled The Roti Rebellion, which was written and directed by Supriya Karunakaran. The play was organized by Sparsh, a theatre group, and presented in June 2005 at The Moving Theatre at Andhra Saraswat Parishad, Hyderabad, Andhra Pradesh.

Samad Iqbal, a fictional descendant of Mangal Pandey, is a central character in Zadie Smith's debut novel White Teeth. Pandey is an important influence on Samad's life and is repeatedly referenced and investigated by the novel's characters.

• Commemoration

1. The Mangal Pandey cenotaph on Surendranath Banerjee road at Barrackpore Cantonment, West Bengal.
2. The Government of India commemorated Pandey by issuing a postage stamp bearing his image on 5 October 1984. The stamp and the accompanying first-day cover were designed by Delhi-based artist C. R. Pakrashi.
3. A park named Shaheed Mangal Pandey Maha Udyan has been set up at Barrackpore to commemorate the place where Pandey attacked British officers and was subsequently hanged.

• Barrackpore mutiny of 1824

Barrackpore (Barrackpur), West Bengal, India

The Barrackpore mutiny was a rising of native Indian sepoys against their British officers in Barrackpore in November 1824. The incident occurred when the British East India Company was fighting the First Anglo-Burmese War (1824–1826) under the leadership of the Governor-General of Bengal, William Amherst, 1st Earl Amherst.

The mutiny had its roots in British insensitivity towards Indian cultural sentiments, combined with negligence and poor supply arrangements, which caused growing resentment amongst the sepoys of several regiments of the Bengal Native Infantry after a long march from Mathura to Barrackpore. The lack of transport for personal effects and cultural concerns about being transported by sea caused apprehension and when troops from the 47th Native Infantry appeared on parade, the troops refused to march towards Chittagong, unless their grievances were remedied. Attempts to resolve the dispute failed and dissent spread to elements of the 26th and 62nd Regiments.

The Commander-in-Chief, India, General Sir Edward Paget, ordered the troops to lay down their arms before considering their requests for redress. When the sepoys refused, their camp was surrounded by loyal soldiers from the 26th and 62nd Regiments and two British regiments. After a final ultimatum, the camp was attacked with artillery and infantry and around 180 sepoys were killed, as were a number of civilian bystanders.

In the aftermath, a number of mutineers were hanged and others sentenced to long periods of penal servitude. The 47th Regiment was disbanded and its Indian officers dismissed, while its European officers were transferred to other regiments. The incident was largely suppressed in the Indian and British media, with only limited information being released to the British public; despite this, there was Parliamentary criticism of the East India Company government for its heavy-handedness in dealing with the sepoys' grievances.

- Prelude

During the First Anglo-Burmese War, in October 1824, the 26th, 47th and 62nd Regiments of the Bengal Native Infantry were ordered to march 500 mi (800 km) from Barrackpore, a military cantonment in Bengal near Calcutta, to Chittagong in preparation for entering Burmese territory. The regiments had just marched almost 1,000 mi (1,600 km) from Mathura to Barrackpore and were reluctant to undertake another long march, this time against the

Burmese, an unknown enemy. Rumours of magical Burmese prowess spread amongst the Indian sepoys, affecting their morale particularly after the Burmese victory at Ramu. Moreover, these three regiments consisted mostly of high caste Hindus, who had reservations about crossing the sea due to the kala pani taboo.

- Immediate causes

Apart from fear and fatigue, what disheartened the sepoys the most was the absence of carriage cattle. Each high caste soldier used his own brass cooking utensils, wrapped in a bundle that also included his bedding. Because of their weight, the bundles could not be carried by the soldiers in addition to their knapsacks, muskets and ammunition. At the time, bullocks were generally used to pull the carts carrying the bundles. For the march to Chittagong, no bullocks could be found, since almost all the available animals had already been purchased for the sea-borne expedition to Rangoon. The few bullocks that were available were of inferior quality and cost exorbitant rates beyond the means of the sepoys, who requested that the government should provide the bullocks or pay them double batta (the allowance paid when in hostile territory) to cover the cost of purchasing them.

These requests were disregarded and the sepoys were instead advised to carry whatever they could in their knapsacks and to leave the rest behind. To resolve the situation, commanding officers offered a 4,000 rupee advance to each regiment. The sepoys turned down this offer as it still meant paying baggage charges out of their own pocket. The situation was escalated by threats from a Muslim Indian subedar major, that if they did not stop complaining about the bullocks, they would be sent by sea.

- Events of the rebellion

A portrait of General Sir Edward Paget, who suppressed the mutiny.

The 26th Regiment was ordered to march first, followed by the 47th and then the 62nd Regiment. In a last moment change of orders, the 47th Regiment was asked to commence the march on 1 November 1824, followed by the other two regiments who were ordered to start within a week of the 47th Regiment's departure. A parade was held on 1 November, during which the soldiers of the 47th Native Infantry appeared without their knapsacks and refused to bring them even when ordered to do so. They again demanded their carriage bullocks or payment of double batta and refused to march without a redress of grievances. The commanding officer, General Dalzell, was unable to subdue the discontent and proceeded to Calcutta to consult the Commander-in-Chief, India, General Sir Edward Paget. The other two regiments were also affected and twenty Indian sepoys from the 26th BNI and 160 from the 62nd BNI defected to the refractory sepoys of the 47th Regiment.

Under the leadership of Bindee Tiwari, the sepoys maintained order during the day and stayed on the parade ground all night, while a petition was sent to Paget, who arrived from Calcutta on hearing of the escalation.

Sepoys presented their demands to Paget via an emissary and explained that their act was due to religious scruples and requested to be dismissed from service, if the demands were not met. Paget replied that legitimate demands would only be addressed after the sepoys laid down their arms. This promise of reconsideration was not enough for the sepoys to give up their position. Paget, an old school martinet of Royal Service, considered this refusal an act of armed mutiny. He summoned two regiments of European troops, the 47th (Lancashire) Regiment of Foot and the 1st (Royal) Regiment, as well as troops of the Governor General's bodyguard from Calcutta. He also brought horse artillery from nearby Dum Dum.

On the morning of 2 November, the reinforcements and the loyal members of the 26th and 62nd Regiments moved into position. They secretly surrounded the sepoy camp ground and a final message was sent to the mutineers, demanding that they lay down arms before any discussion on grievances but it is said that only ten minutes were offered to make up their minds. The sepoys either hesitated or rejected the ultimatum and Paget ordered two cannons to fire on the rebels, followed by an attack from the rear by the secretly placed horse artillery. Surprised by this sudden assault, the sepoys tried to flee but the rest of the British regiments attacked from all directions. Some of the sepoys jumped into the Hooghly River to escape and drowned, others entered local households for shelter but the loyalists chased them in and killed them with bayonets. Many bystanders, including women and children who happened to be in the neighbourhood, were killed during the operation. Afterwards, it was found that the muskets of the Indian sepoys were not loaded. Stevenson concludes that this implies no violence was intended by the rebels.

- Casualties

Of about 1,400 mutineers, 180 were killed during the attack, although the death toll is disputed. Bengal Hurkaru, a local semi-official newspaper, published a report in November 1824, stating that the number of deceased was 100, per a "perfect guess". In 1827, Joseph Hume, an opposition MP, reported on the floor of the British Parliament that the number was from 400–600 per the "facts that had reached him from India". In response Charles Williams-Wynn, a Tory MP, claimed on behalf of the government, that the number was no more than 180.

- After Punishment of the mutineers

Most of the remaining mutineers were captured and on 2 November, eleven sepoys were identified as the ring leaders and received a swift trial, where they were sentenced to death by hanging. Six of these were from 47th BNI, four were from 62nd BNI and one was from 26th BNI, who were killed the same day in the parade ground. Around 52 sepoys were sentenced to fourteen years' hard labour, in chains, on roads; numerous others were sentenced with lesser terms. On 4 November, by a general order issued from Fort William, the 47th Regiment was disbanded and its Indian officers disgraced, discharged and declared unworthy of the confidence of the government, as it was thought mutiny could not have occurred without their knowledge. All the British officers were transferred to a new 69th Regiment. On 9 November, Bindee was arrested nearby, and suffered the especially harsh punishment of being hung in chains on the next day. His body was left to rot for months in open public display.

- Earl Amherst, Governor General of India, was harshly criticised by a British newspaper report.

The news of the unrest in Barrackpore, especially concerning the use of violence to subdue a peaceful protest, was suppressed in public media in Calcutta, London and elsewhere. The colonial government maintained its silence except for a short official paragraph published in the Calcutta Gazette on 4 November, where the incident was largely trivialised, with no mention of casualties. Bengal Hurkaru, a local semi-official newspaper under the editorship of a British Deputy Judge-Advocate, also published a short report in November 1824. The report played down the incident and lacked basic details including the cause of the mutiny, stating that they were not allowed to publish such details. Apart from these two reports, common Indians and Britons were largely kept uninformed about the incident, although rumours circulated.

- Later criticism in press

The Oriental Herald in London first published a story on the subject almost six months after the incident, calling it the "Barrackpore Massacre", based on a report by a British correspondent in Calcutta. The Oriental Herald severely criticised the conduct of the British officers present, Paget in particular for resorting to violence to suppress a peaceful protest, and demanded increased pay for the sepoys as well the provision of transport for luggage. It also sought a consistent and truthful account of the incident from the government. The report was particularly harsh in its criticism of Amherst, whom it labelled an "evil genius", blaming him for the escalation.

If this example was necessary to preserve the obedience of the native troops, how miserably precarious is the tenure of our authority! If it was not necessary, may God forgive those who have brought this stain upon British name.Barrackpore Massacre – Burmese War – Present State of the Native Army in Bengal, The Oriental Herald, Volume 5, 1825.

- Consequences

After the suppression of the mutiny, many sepoys deserted British service. A Court of Inquiry was set up to investigate the incident. All that is known about its report was that it agreed that the sepoys had justifiable grievances. Bengal units designated for 'General Service' were given all the concessions that the rebellious sepoys had originally demanded. The 1824 incident created an atmosphere of distrust across the native Indian regiments and irrevocably harmed relations between British officers and native Indian sepoys.

No disciplinary measures were taken against Paget or any other officer of the army, contrary to expectations.Amherst came close to being recalled for mishandling the situation but ultimately retained his position.

- Debate in British Parliament

On 22 March 1827, a parliamentary debate in the House of Commons discussed the Barrackpore Mutiny. Hume, a Radical MP from the opposition, described the incident to his colleagues, criticising the conduct of the military, and appealed for a fresh investigation to identify those responsible; he perceived that Amherst was showing a lack of will in finding the real culprits. He also alleged that the report of the Court of Inquiry was being suppressed, demanded that the full report be produced in Parliament, and appealed for the House to hear both sides of the dispute and come to a just conclusion. Tory MPs from the government side, such as Wynn and Davies, objected to the proposal and supported Amherst and Paget. At the end of the debate, the motion for a fresh investigation and the presentation of the inquiry's report to the House was defeated, 44 votes for the motion and 176 against.

- Historical significance

Mangal Pandey, another sepoy, was involved in a subsequent incident at Barrackpore that contributed to the Indian rebellion of 1857.

The Barrackpore cantonment was the site of another mutinous incident thirty-three years later on 29 March 1857 involving sepoy Mangal Pandey. The 24th Chief of Army Staff of the Indian Army, Major General V.K. Singh (2010–2012), wrote extensively about the 1824 Barrackpore mutiny. He reflects:

What shocked everyone was not the mutiny itself but the brutal manner in which it was quelled. The bloodshed could have been avoided if the situation had been handled with tact and understanding by the officers, particularly General Paget. Though the mutiny was quickly suppressed – it lasted for less than a day – its long term effects were far reaching and had a bearing on the Great Indian Mutiny of 1857.Gen V.K. Singh, Barrackpore Mutiny, Contribution of the Armed Forces to the Freedom Movement in India

The events of 1824 continued to haunt Britons and Indians for many years and many felt that it provided Indian sepoys the rationale to kill British officers in 1857.

- Memorial

Bindee became a martyr and a fabled hero among the Indian sepoys especially after his death. To commemorate the incident, six months after Bindee's death, Indian sepoys and locals erected a temple near the site of his execution. Binda Baba temple as it is now known, still stands.

TWO

INDIAN REBELLION OF 1857

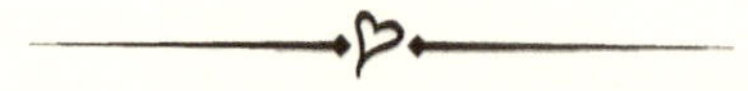

As many as 800,000 Indians and possibly more, both in the rebellion and in famines and epidemics of disease in its wake, by comparison of 1857 population estimates with Indian Census of 1871.

The Indian Rebellion of 1857 was a major uprising in India in 1857–58 against the rule of the British East India Company, which functioned as a sovereign power on behalf of the British Crown. The rebellion began on 10 May 1857 in the form of a mutiny of sepoys of the Company's army in the garrison town of Meerut, 40 mi (64 km) northeast of Delhi. It then erupted into other mutinies and civilian rebellions chiefly in the upper Gangetic plain and central India, though incidents of revolt also occurred farther north and east. The rebellion posed a considerable threat to British power in that region, and was contained only with the rebels' defeat in Gwalior on 20 June 1858.

On 1 November 1858, the British granted amnesty to all rebels not involved in murder, though they did not declare the hostilities to have formally ended until 8 July 1859. Its name is contested, and it is variously described as the Sepoy Mutiny, the Indian Mutiny, the Great Rebellion, the Revolt of 1857, the Indian Insurrection, and the First War of Independence.

The Indian rebellion was fed by resentments born of diverse perceptions, including invasive British-style social reforms, harsh land taxes, summary treatment of some rich landowners and princes, as well as scepticism about the improvements brought about by British rule. Many Indians rose against the British; however, many also fought for the British, and the majority remained seemingly compliant to British rule. Violence, which sometimes betrayed exceptional cruelty, was inflicted on both sides, on British officers, and civilians, including women and children, by the rebels, and on the rebels, and their supporters, including sometimes entire villages, by British reprisals; the cities of Delhi and Lucknow were laid waste in the fighting and the British retaliation.

After the outbreak of the mutiny in Meerut, the rebels quickly reached Delhi, whose 81-year-old Mughal ruler, Bahadur Shah Zafar, was declared the Emperor of Hindustan. Soon, the rebels had captured large tracts of the North-Western Provinces and Awadh (Oudh). The East India Company's response came rapidly as well. With help from reinforcements, Kanpur was retaken by mid-July 1857, and Delhi by the end of September.However, it then took the remainder of 1857 and the better part of 1858 for the rebellion to be suppressed in Jhansi, Lucknow, and especially the Awadh countryside.

Other regions of Company-controlled India—Bengal province, the Bombay Presidency, and the Madras Presidency—remained largely calm. In Assam, a plan to reinstate the Ahom kingdom taking advantage of the situation elsewhere in India was set up, but it died off with the hanging of Maniram Dewan and Piyali Barua, and the subsequent forceful crushing of public reaction. In the Punjab, the Sikh princes crucially helped the British by providing both soldiers and support. The large princely states, Hyderabad, Mysore, Travancore, and Kashmir, as well as the smaller ones of Rajputana, did not join the rebellion, serving the British, in the Governor-General Lord Canning's words, as "breakwaters in a storm."

In some regions, most notably in Awadh, the rebellion took on the attributes of a patriotic revolt against British oppression. However, the rebel leaders proclaimed no articles of faith that presaged a new political system. Even so, the rebellion proved to be an important watershed in Indian and British Empire history. It led to the dissolution of the East India Company, and forced the British to reorganize the army, the financial system, and the administration in India, through passage of the Government of India Act 1858. India was thereafter administered directly by the British government in the new British Raj. On 1 November 1858, Queen Victoria issued a proclamation to Indians, which while lacking the authority of a constitutional provision, promised rights similar to those of other British subjects. In the following decades, when admission to these rights was not always forthcoming, Indians were to pointedly refer to the Queen's proclamation in growing avowals of a new nationalism.

- India in 1837 and 1857, showing East India Company-governed territories in pink

Although the British East India Company had established a presence in India as far back as 1612, and earlier administered the factory areas established for trading purposes, its victory in the Battle of Plassey in 1757 marked the beginning of its firm foothold in eastern India. The victory was consolidated in 1764 at the Battle of Buxar, when the East India Company army defeated Mughal Emperor Shah Alam II. After his defeat, the emperor granted the Company the right to the "collection of Revenue" in the provinces of Bengal (modern day Bengal, Bihar, and Odisha), known as "Diwani" to the Company. The Company soon expanded its territories around its bases in Bombay and Madras; later, the Anglo-Mysore Wars (1766–1799) and the Anglo-Maratha Wars (1772–1818) led to control of even more of India.

In 1806, the Vellore Mutiny was sparked by new uniform regulations that created resentment amongst both Hindu and Muslim sepoys.

After the turn of the 19th century, Governor-General Wellesley began what became two decades of accelerated expansion of Company territories. This was achieved either by subsidiary alliances between the Company and local rulers or by direct military annexation. The subsidiary alliances created the princely states of the Hindu maharajas and the Muslim nawabs. Punjab, North-West Frontier Province, and Kashmir were annexed after the Second Anglo-Sikh War in 1849; however, Kashmir was immediately sold under the 1846 Treaty of Amritsar to the Dogra Dynasty of Jammu and thereby became a princely state. The border dispute between Nepal and British India, which sharpened after 1801, had caused the Anglo-Nepalese War of 1814–16 and brought the defeated Gurkhas under British influence. In 1854, Berar was annexed, and the state of Oudh was added two years later. For practical purposes, the Company was the government of much of India.

- Causes of the rebellion

The Indian Rebellion of 1857 occurred as the result of an accumulation of factors over time, rather than any single event.

The sepoys were Indian soldiers who were recruited into the Company's army. Just before the rebellion, there were over 300,000 sepoys in the army, compared to about 50,000 British. The forces were divided into three presidency armies: Bombay, Madras, and Bengal. The Bengal Army recruited higher castes, such as Brahmins, Rajputs and Bhumihar, mostly from the Awadh and Bihar regions, and even restricted the enlistment of lower castes in 1855.In contrast, the Madras Army and Bombay Army were "more localized, caste-neutral armies" that "did not prefer high-caste men".The domination of higher castes in the Bengal Army has been blamed in part for initial mutinies that led to the rebellion.

- Two sepoy officers; a private sepoy, 1820s

In 1772, when Warren Hastings was appointed India's first Governor-General, one of his first undertakings was the rapid expansion of the Company's army. Since the sepoys from Bengal – many of whom had fought against the Company in the Battles of Plassey and Buxar – were now suspect in British eyes, Hastings recruited farther west from the high-caste rural Rajputs and Bhumihar of Awadh and Bihar, a practice that continued for the next 75 years.

However, in order to forestall any social friction, the Company also took action to adapt its military practices to the requirements of their religious rituals. Consequently, these soldiers dined in separate facilities; in addition, overseas service, considered polluting to their caste, was not required of them, and the army soon came officially to recognise Hindu festivals. "This encouragement of high caste ritual status, however, left the government vulnerable to protest, even mutiny, whenever the sepoys detected infringement of their prerogatives." Stokes argues that "The British scrupulously avoided interference with the social structure of the village community which remained largely intact."

After the annexation of Oudh (Awadh) by the East India Company in 1856, many sepoys were disquieted both from losing their perquisites, as landed gentry, in the Oudh courts, and from the anticipation of any increased land-revenue payments that the annexation might bring about. Other historians have stressed that by 1857, some Indian soldiers, interpreting the presence of missionaries as a sign of official intent, were convinced that the Company was masterminding mass conversions of Hindus and Muslims to Christianity. Although earlier in the 1830s, evangelicals such as William Carey and William Wilberforce had successfully clamoured for the passage of social reform, such as the abolition of sati and allowing the remarriage of Hindu widows, there is little evidence that the sepoys' allegiance was affected by this.

However, changes in the terms of their professional service may have created resentment. As the extent of the East India Company's jurisdiction expanded with victories in wars or annexation, the soldiers were now expected not only to serve in less familiar regions, such as in Burma, but also to make do without the "foreign service" remuneration that had previously been their due.

A major cause of resentment that arose ten months prior to the outbreak of the rebellion was the General Service Enlistment Act of 25 July 1856. As noted above, men of the Bengal Army had been exempted from overseas service. Specifically, they were enlisted only for service in territories to which they could march. Governor-General Lord Dalhousie saw this as an anomaly, since all sepoys of the Madras and Bombay Armies and the six "General Service" battalions of the Bengal Army had accepted an obligation to serve overseas if required. As a result, the burden of providing contingents for active service in Burma, readily accessible only by sea, and China had fallen disproportionately on the two smaller Presidency Armies. As signed into effect by Lord Canning, Dalhousie's successor as Governor-General, the act required only new recruits to the Bengal Army to accept a commitment for general service. However, serving high-caste sepoys were fearful that it would be eventually extended to them, as well as preventing sons following fathers into an army with a strong tradition of family service.

There were also grievances over the issue of promotions, based on seniority. This, as well as the increasing number of British officers in the battalions, made promotion slow, and many Indian officers did not reach commissioned rank until they were too old to be effective.

- The Enfield rifle

The final spark was provided by the ammunition for the new Enfield Pattern 1853 rifled musket.These rifles, which fired Minié balls, had a tighter fit than the earlier muskets, and used paper cartridges that came pre-greased. To load the rifle, sepoys had to bite the cartridge open to release the powder.The grease used on these cartridges was rumoured to include tallow derived from beef, which would be offensive to Hindus, and lard derived from pork, which would be offensive to Muslims. At least one Company official pointed out the difficulties this might cause:

unless it be proven that the grease employed in these cartridges is not of a nature to offend or interfere with the prejudices of religion, it will be expedient not to issue them for test to Native corps.

However, in August 1856, greased cartridge production was initiated at Fort William, Calcutta, following a British design. The grease used included tallow supplied by the Indian firm of Gangadarh Banerji & Co. By January, rumours abounded that the Enfield cartridges were greased with animal fat.

Company officers became aware of the rumours through reports of an altercation between a high-caste sepoy and a low-caste labourer at Dum Dum. The labourer had taunted the sepoy that by biting the cartridge, he had himself lost caste, although at this time such cartridges had been issued only at Meerut and not at Dum Dum. There had been rumours that the British sought to destroy the religions of the Indian people, and forcing the native soldiers to break their sacred code would have certainly added to this rumour, as it apparently did. The Company was quick to reverse the effects of this policy in hopes that the unrest would be quelled.

On 27 January, Colonel Richard Birch, the Military Secretary, ordered that all cartridges issued from depots were to be free from grease, and that sepoys could grease them themselves using whatever mixture "they may prefer". A modification was also made to the drill for loading so that the cartridge was torn with the hands and not bitten.

This, however, merely caused many sepoys to be convinced that the rumours were true and that their fears were justified. Additional rumours started that the paper in the new cartridges, which was glazed and stiffer than the previously used paper, was impregnated with grease. In February, a court of inquiry was held at Barrackpore to get to the bottom of these rumours. Native soldiers called as witnesses complained of the paper "being stiff and like cloth in the mode of tearing", said that when the paper was burned it smelled of grease, and announced that the suspicion that the paper itself contained grease could not be removed from their minds.

• Civilian disquiet

Civilian rebellion was more multifarious. The rebels consisted of three groups: the feudal nobility, rural landlords called taluqdars, and the peasants. The nobility, many of whom had lost titles and domains under the Doctrine of Lapse, which refused to recognise the adopted children of princes as legal heirs, felt that the Company had interfered with a traditional system of inheritance. Rebel leaders such as Nana Sahib and the Rani of Jhansi belonged to this group; the latter, for example, was prepared to accept East India Company supremacy if her adopted son was recognised as her late husband's heir. In other areas of central India, such as Indore and Saugar, where such loss of privilege had not occurred, the princes remained loyal to the Company, even in areas where the sepoys had rebelled.

The second group, the taluqdars, had lost half their landed estates to peasant farmers as a result of the land reforms that came in the wake of annexation of Oudh. It is mentioned that throughout Oudh till Bihar Rajput Taluqdars provided the bulk of leadership and played an important role during 1857 in the region.As the rebellion gained ground, the taluqdars quickly reoccupied the lands they had lost, and paradoxically, in part because of ties of kinship and feudal loyalty, did not experience significant opposition from the peasant farmers, many of whom joined the rebellion, to the great dismay of the British.

It has also been suggested that heavy land-revenue assessment in some areas by the British resulted in many landowning families either losing their land or going into great debt to money lenders, and providing ultimately a reason to rebel; money lenders, in addition to the Company, were particular objects of the rebels' animosity. The civilian rebellion was also highly uneven in its geographic distribution, even in areas of north-central India that were no longer under British control. For example, the relatively prosperous Muzaffarnagar district, a beneficiary of a Company irrigation scheme, and next door to Meerut, where the upheaval began, stayed relatively calm throughout.

Bahadur Shah Zafar, the last Mughal Emperor, crowned Emperor of India, by the Indian troops, he was deposed by the British, and died in exile in Burma

"Utilitarian and evangelical-inspired social reform", including the abolition of sati and the legalisation of widow remarriage were considered by many—especially the British themselves—to have caused suspicion that Indian religious traditions were being "interfered with", with the ultimate aim of conversion.

Recent historians, including Chris Bayly, have preferred to frame this as a "clash of knowledges", with proclamations from religious authorities before the revolt and testimony after it including on such issues as the "insults to women", the rise of "low persons under British tutelage", the "pollution" caused by Western medicine and the persecuting and ignoring of traditional astrological authorities. British-run schools were also a problem: according to recorded testimonies, anger had spread because of stories that mathematics was replacing religious instruction, stories were chosen that would "bring contempt" upon Indian religions, and because girl children were exposed to "moral danger" by education.

The justice system was considered to be inherently unfair to the Indians. The official Blue Books, East India (Torture) 1855–1857, laid before the House of Commons during the sessions of 1856 and 1857, revealed that Company officers were allowed an extended series of appeals if convicted or accused of brutality or crimes against Indians.The economic policies of the East India Company were also resented by many Indians.

· The Bengal Army

Each of the three "Presidencies" into which the East India Company divided India for administrative purposes maintained their own armies. Of these, the Army of the Bengal Presidency was the largest. Unlike the other two, it recruited heavily from among high-caste Hindus and comparatively wealthy Muslims. The Muslims formed a larger percentage of the 18 irregular cavalry units within the Bengal Army, whilst Hindus were mainly to be found in the 84 regular infantry and cavalry regiments. The sepoys were therefore affected to a large degree by the concerns of the landholding and traditional members of Indian society. In the early years of Company rule, it tolerated and even encouraged the caste privileges and customs within the Bengal Army, which recruited its regular soldiers almost exclusively amongst the landowning Rajputs and Brahmins of the Bihar and Awadh regions. These soldiers were known as Purbiyas. By the time these customs and privileges came to be threatened by modernising regimes in Calcutta from the 1840s onwards, the sepoys had become accustomed to very high ritual status and were extremely sensitive to suggestions that their caste might be polluted.

The sepoys also gradually became dissatisfied with various other aspects of army life. Their pay was relatively low and after Awadh and the Punjab were annexed, the soldiers no longer received extra pay (batta or bhatta) for service there, because they were no longer considered "foreign missions". The junior British officers became increasingly estranged from their soldiers, in many cases treating them as their racial inferiors. In 1856, a new Enlistment Act was introduced by the Company, which in theory made every unit in the Bengal Army liable to service overseas. Although it was intended to apply only to new recruits, the serving sepoys feared that the Act might be applied retroactively to them as well. A high-caste Hindu who travelled in the cramped conditions of a wooden troop ship could not cook his own food on his own fire, and accordingly risked losing caste through ritual pollution.

· Onset of the rebellion

Indian mutiny map showing position of troops on 1 May 1857
Several months of increasing tensions coupled with various incidents preceded the actual rebellion. On 26 February 1857 the 19th Bengal Native Infantry (BNI) regiment became concerned that new cartridges they had been issued were wrapped in paper greased with cow and pig fat, which had to be opened by mouth thus affecting their religious sensibilities. Their Colonel confronted them supported by artillery and cavalry on the parade ground, but after some negotiation withdrew the artillery, and cancelled the next morning's parade.

· Mangal Pandey

On 29 March 1857 at the Barrackpore parade ground, near Calcutta, 29-year-old Mangal Pandey of the 34th BNI, angered by the recent actions of the East India Company, declared that he would rebel against his commanders. Informed about Pandey's behaviour Sergeant-Major James Hewson went to investigate, only to have Pandey shoot at him. Hewson raised the alarm.When his adjutant Lt. Henry Baugh came out to investigate the unrest, Pandey opened fire but hit Baugh's horse instead.

General John Hearsey came out to the parade ground to investigate, and claimed later that Mangal Pandey was in some kind of "religious frenzy". He ordered the Indian commander of the quarter guard Jemadar Ishwari Prasad to arrest Mangal Pandey, but the Jemadar refused. The quarter guard and other sepoys present, with the single exception of a soldier called Shaikh Paltu, drew back from restraining or arresting Mangal Pandey. Shaikh Paltu restrained Pandey from continuing his attack.

After failing to incite his comrades into an open and active rebellion, Mangal Pandey tried to take his own life, by placing his musket to his chest and pulling the trigger with his toe. He managed only to wound himself. He was court-martialled on 6 April, and hanged two days later.

The Jemadar Ishwari Prasad was sentenced to death and hanged on 21 April. The regiment was disbanded and stripped of its uniforms because it was felt that it harboured ill-feelings towards its superiors, particularly after this incident. Shaikh Paltu was promoted to the rank of havildar in the Bengal Army, but was murdered shortly before the 34th BNI dispersed.

Sepoys in other regiments thought these punishments were harsh. The demonstration of disgrace during the formal disbanding helped foment the rebellion in view of some historians. Disgruntled ex-sepoys returned home to Awadh with a desire for revenge.

• Unrest during April 1857

During April, there was unrest and fires at Agra, Allahabad and Ambala. At Ambala in particular, which was a large military cantonment where several units had been collected for their annual musketry practice, it was clear to General Anson, Commander-in-Chief of the Bengal Army, that some sort of rebellion over the cartridges was imminent. Despite the objections of the civilian Governor-General's staff, he agreed to postpone the musketry practice and allow a new drill by which the soldiers tore the cartridges with their fingers rather than their teeth. However, he issued no general orders making this standard practice throughout the Bengal Army and, rather than remain at Ambala to defuse or overawe potential trouble, he then proceeded to Simla, the cool "hill station" where many high officials spent the summer.

Although there was no open revolt at Ambala, there was widespread arson during late April. Barrack buildings (especially those belonging to soldiers who had used the Enfield cartridges) and British officers' bungalows were set on fire.

• Meerut

"The Sepoy revolt at Meerut," wood-engraving from the Illustrated London News, 1857An 1858 photograph by Felice Beato of a mosque in Meerut where some of the rebel soldiers may have prayed

At Meerut, a large military cantonment, 2,357 Indian sepoys and 2,038 British soldiers were stationed along with 12 British-manned guns. The station held one of the largest concentrations of British troops in India and this was later to be cited as evidence that the original rising was a spontaneous outbreak rather than a pre-planned plot.

Although the state of unrest within the Bengal Army was well known, on 24 April Lieutenant Colonel George Carmichael-Smyth, the unsympathetic commanding officer of the 3rd Bengal Light Cavalry, ordered 90 of his men to parade and perform firing drills. All except five of the men on parade refused to accept their cartridges. On 9 May, the remaining 85 men were court martialled, and most were sentenced to 10 years' imprisonment with hard labour. Eleven comparatively young soldiers were given five years' imprisonment. The entire garrison was paraded and watched as the condemned men were stripped of their uniforms and placed in shackles. As they were marched off to jail, the condemned soldiers berated their comrades for failing to support them.

The next day was Sunday. Some Indian soldiers warned off-duty junior British officers that plans were afoot to release the imprisoned soldiers by force, but the senior officers to whom this was reported took no action. There was also unrest in the city of Meerut itself, with angry protests in the bazaar and some buildings being set on fire. In the evening, most British officers were preparing to attend church, while many of the British soldiers were off duty and had gone into canteens or into the bazaar in Meerut. The Indian troops, led by the 3rd Cavalry, broke into revolt. British junior officers who attempted to quell the first outbreaks were killed by the rebels.

British officers' and civilians' quarters were attacked, and four civilian men, eight women and eight children were killed. Crowds in the bazaar attacked off-duty soldiers there. About 50 Indian civilians, some of them officers' servants who tried to defend or conceal their employers, were killed by the sepoys. While the action of the sepoys in freeing their 85 imprisoned comrades appears to have been spontaneous, some civilian rioting in the city was reportedly encouraged by kotwal (local police commander) Dhan Singh Gurjar.

Some sepoys (especially from the 11th Bengal Native Infantry) escorted trusted British officers and women and children to safety before joining the revolt. Some officers and their families escaped to Rampur, where they found refuge with the Nawab.

The British historian Philip Mason notes that it was inevitable that most of the sepoys and sowars from Meerut should have made for Delhi on the night of 10 May. It was a strong walled city located only forty miles away, it was the ancient capital and present seat of the nominal Mughal Emperor and finally there were no British troops in garrison there in contrast to Meerut. No effort was made to pursue them.

- Wood-engraving depicting the massacre of officers by insurgent cavalry at Delhi

Early on 11 May, the first parties of the 3rd Cavalry reached Delhi. From beneath the windows of the King's apartments in the palace, they called on Bahadur Shah to acknowledge and lead them. He did nothing at this point, apparently treating the sepoys as ordinary petitioners, but others in the palace were quick to join the revolt. During the day, the revolt spread. British officials and dependents, Indian Christians and shop keepers within the city were killed, some by sepoys and others by crowds of rioters.

The Flagstaff Tower, Delhi, where the British survivors of the rebellion gathered on 11 May 1857; photographed by Felice Beato

There were three battalion-sized regiments of Bengal Native Infantry stationed in or near the city. Some detachments quickly joined the rebellion, while others held back but also refused to obey orders to take action against the rebels. In the afternoon, a violent explosion in the city was heard for several miles. Fearing that the arsenal, which contained large stocks of arms and ammunition, would fall intact into rebel hands, the nine British Ordnance officers there had opened fire on the sepoys, including the men of their own guard. When resistance appeared hopeless, they blew up the arsenal. Six of the nine officers survived, but the blast killed many in the streets and nearby houses and other buildings.

The news of these events finally tipped the sepoys stationed around Delhi into open rebellion. The sepoys were later able to salvage at least some arms from the arsenal, and a magazine two miles (3 km) outside Delhi, containing up to 3,000 barrels of gunpowder, was captured without resistance.

Many fugitive British officers and civilians had congregated at the Flagstaff Tower on the ridge north of Delhi, where telegraph operators were sending news of the events to other British stations. When it became clear that the help expected from Meerut was not coming, they made their way in carriages to Karnal. Those who became separated from the main body or who could not reach the Flagstaff Tower also set out for Karnal on foot. Some were helped by villagers on the way; others were killed.

The next day, Bahadur Shah held his first formal court for many years. It was attended by many excited sepoys. The King was alarmed by the turn events had taken, but eventually accepted the sepoys' allegiance and agreed to give his countenance to the rebellion. On 16 May, up to 50 British who had been held prisoner in the palace or had been discovered hiding in the city were killed by some of the King's servants under a peepul tree in a courtyard outside the palace.

· States during the rebellion

The news of the events at Meerut and Delhi spread rapidly, provoking uprisings among sepoys and disturbances in many districts. In many cases, it was the behaviour of British military and civilian authorities themselves which precipitated disorder. Learning of the fall of Delhi, many Company administrators hastened to remove themselves, their families and servants to places of safety. At Agra, 160 miles (260 km) from Delhi, no fewer than 6,000 assorted non-combatants converged on the Fort.

The military authorities also reacted in disjointed manner. Some officers trusted their sepoys, but others tried to disarm them to forestall potential uprisings. At Benares and Allahabad, the disarmings were bungled, also leading to local revolts.

· Troops of the Native Allies by George Francklin Atkinson, 1859

In 1857, the Bengal Army had 86,000 men, of which 12,000 were British, 16,000 Sikh and 1,500 Gurkha. There were 311,000 native soldiers in India altogether, 40,160 British soldiers (including units of the British Army) and 5,362 officers. Fifty-four of the Bengal Army's 74 regular Native Infantry Regiments mutinied, but some were immediately destroyed or broke up, with their sepoys drifting away to their homes. A number of the remaining 20 regiments were disarmed or disbanded to prevent or forestall mutiny. Only twelve of the original Bengal Native Infantry regiments survived to pass into the new Indian Army. All ten of the Bengal Light Cavalry regiments mutinied.

The Bengal Army also contained 29 irregular cavalry and 42 irregular infantry regiments. Of these, a substantial contingent from the recently annexed state of Awadh mutinied en masse. Another large contingent from Gwalior also mutinied, even though that state's ruler (Jayajirao Scindia) supported the British. The remainder of the irregular units were raised from a wide variety of sources and were less affected by the concerns of mainstream Indian society. Some irregular units actively supported the Company: three Gurkha and five of six Sikh infantry units, and the six infantry and six cavalry units of the recently raised Punjab Irregular Force.

On 1 April 1858, the number of Indian soldiers in the Bengal army loyal to the Company was 80,053. However large numbers were hastily raised in the Punjab and North-West Frontier after the outbreak of the Rebellion.

The Bombay army had three mutinies in its 29 regiments, whilst the Madras army had none at all, although elements of one of its 52 regiments refused to volunteer for service in Bengal.[98] Nonetheless, most of southern India remained passive, with only intermittent outbreaks of violence. Many parts of the region were ruled by the Nizams or the Mysore royalty, and were thus not directly under British rule.

Most Muslims did not share the rebels' dislike of the British administration and their ulema could not agree on whether to declare a jihad. There were Islamic scholars such as Maulana Muhammad Qasim Nanautavi and Maulana Rashid Ahmad Gangohi who took up arms against the colonial rule, but many Muslims, among them ulema from both the Sunni and Shia sects, sided with the British. Various Ahl-i-Hadith scholars and colleagues of Nanautavi rejected the jihad. The most influential member of Ahl-i-Hadith ulema in Delhi, Maulana Sayyid Nazir Husain Dehlvi, resisted pressure from the mutineers to call for a jihad and instead declared in favour of British rule, viewing the Muslim-British relationship as a legal contract which could not be broken unless their religious rights were breached.

Although most of the mutinous sepoys in Delhi were Hindus, a significant proportion of the insurgents were Muslims. The proportion of ghazis grew to be about a quarter of the local fighting force by the end of the siege and included a regiment of suicide ghazis from Gwalior who had vowed never to eat again and to fight until they met certain death at the hands of British troops.

The Sikhs and Pathans of the Punjab and North-West Frontier Province supported the British and helped in the recapture of Delhi. Historian John Harris has asserted that the Sikhs wanted to avenge the annexation of the Sikh Empire eight years earlier by the Company with the help of Purbiyas ('Easterners'), Biharis and those from the United Provinces of Agra and Oudh who had formed part of the East India Company's armies in the First and Second Anglo-Sikh Wars. He has also suggested that Sikhs felt insulted by the attitude of sepoys who, in the Sikhs' view, had beaten the Khalsa only with British help; they resented and despised them far more than they did the British.

• Sikh Troops Dividing the Spoil Taken from Mutineers, circa 1860

The Sikhs feared reinstatement of Mughal rule in northern India because they had been persecuted heavily in the past by the Mughal dynasty.

Sikh support for the British resulted from grievances surrounding sepoys' perceived conduct during and after the Anglo-Sikh Wars. Firstly, many Sikhs resented that Hindustanis/Purbiyas in service of the Sikh state had been foremost in urging the wars, which lost them their independence. Sikh soldiers also recalled that the bloodiest battles of the war, Chillianwala and Ferozeshah, were won by British troops, and they believed that the Hindustani sepoys had refused to meet them in battle. These feelings were compounded when Hindustani sepoys were assigned a very visible role as garrison troops in Punjab and awarded profit-making civil posts in Punjab.

• Fugitive British officers and their families attacked by mutineers.

A wood-engraving of Nynee Tal (today Nainital) and accompanying story in the Illustrated London News, 15 August 1857, describing how the resort town in the Himalayas served as a refuge for British families escaping from the rebellion of 1857 in Delhi and Meerut.

Bahadur Shah Zafar was proclaimed the Emperor of the whole of India. Most contemporary and modern accounts suggest that he was coerced by the sepoys and his courtiers to sign the proclamation against his will. In spite of the significant loss of power that the Mughal dynasty had suffered in the preceding centuries, their name still carried great prestige across northern India.

Civilians, nobility and other dignitaries took an oath of allegiance. The emperor issued coins in his name, one of the oldest ways of asserting imperial status. The adhesion of the Mughal emperor, however, turned the Sikhs of the Punjab away from the rebellion, as they did not want to return to Islamic rule, having fought many wars against the Mughal rulers. The province of Bengal was largely quiet throughout the entire period. The British, who had long ceased to take the authority of the Mughal Emperor seriously, were astonished at how the ordinary people responded to Zafar's call for war.

Initially, the Indian rebels were able to push back Company forces, and captured several important towns in Haryana, Bihar, the Central Provinces and the United Provinces. When British troops were reinforced and began to counterattack, the mutineers were especially handicapped by their lack of centralized command and control. Although the rebels produced some natural leaders such as Bakht Khan, whom the Emperor later nominated as commander-in-chief after his son Mirza Mughal proved ineffectual, for the most part they were forced to look for leadership to rajahs and princes. Some of these were to prove dedicated leaders, but others were self-interested or inept.

- Attack of the mutineers on the Redan Battery at Lucknow, 30 July 1857

In the countryside around Meerut, a general Gurjar uprising posed the largest threat to the British. In Parikshitgarh near Meerut, Gurjars declared Choudhari Kadam Singh (Kuddum Singh) their leader, and expelled Company police. Kadam Singh Gurjar led a large force, estimates varying from 2,000 to 10,000. Bulandshahr and Bijnor also came under the control of Gurjars under Walidad Khan and Maho Singh respectively. Contemporary sources report that nearly all the Gurjar villages between Meerut and Delhi participated in the revolt, in some cases with support from Jullundur, and it was not until late July that, with the help of local Jats, and the princely states so the British managed to regain control of the area.

The Imperial Gazetteer of India states that throughout the Indian Rebellion of 1857, Gurjars and Ranghars (Muslim rajputs) proved the "most irreconcilable enemies" of the British in the Bulandshahr area.

Mufti Nizamuddin, a renowned scholar of Lahore, issued a Fatwa against the British forces and called upon the local population to support the forces of Rao Tula Ram. Casualties were high at the subsequent engagement at Narnaul (Nasibpur). After the defeat of Rao Tula Ram on 16 November 1857, Mufti Nizamuddin was arrested, and his brother Mufti Yaqinuddin and brother-in-law Abdur Rahman (alias Nabi Baksh) were arrested in Tijara. They were taken to Delhi and hanged.

- Siege of Delhi

Assault on Delhi and capture of the Cashmere Gate, 14 September 1857
The British were slow to strike back at first. It took time for troops stationed in Britain to make their way to India by sea, although some regiments moved overland through Persia from the Crimean War, and some regiments already en route for China were diverted to India.

- Capture of Delhi 1857.

It took time to organise the British troops already in India into field forces, but eventually two columns left Meerut and Simla. They proceeded slowly towards Delhi and fought, killed, and hanged numerous Indians along the way. Two months after the first outbreak of rebellion at Meerut, the two forces met near Karnal. The combined force, including two Gurkha units serving in the Bengal Army under contract from the Kingdom of Nepal, fought the rebels' main army at Badli-ke-Serai and drove them back to Delhi.

The Company's army established a base on the Delhi ridge to the north of the city and the Siege of Delhi began. The siege lasted roughly from 1 July to 21 September. However, the encirclement was hardly complete, and for much of the siege the besiegers were outnumbered and it often seemed that it was the Company forces and not Delhi that were under siege, as the rebels could easily receive resources and reinforcements. For several weeks, it seemed likely that disease, exhaustion and continuous sorties by rebels from Delhi would force the besiegers to withdraw, but the outbreaks of rebellion in the Punjab were forestalled or suppressed, allowing the Punjab Movable Column of British, Sikh and Pakhtun soldiers under John Nicholson to reinforce the besiegers on the Ridge on 14 August. On 30 August the rebels offered terms, which were refused.

- Bank of Delhi was attacked by mortar and gunfire

An eagerly awaited heavy siege train joined the besieging force, and from 7 September, the siege guns battered breaches in the walls and silenced the rebels' artillery.478 An attempt to storm the city through the breaches and the Kashmiri Gate was launched on 14 September.480 The attackers gained a foothold within the city but suffered heavy casualties, including John Nicholson. The British commander (Major General Archdale Wilson) wished to withdraw, but was persuaded to hold on by his junior officers. After a week of street fighting, the British reached the Red Fort. Bahadur Shah Zafar had already fled to Humayun's tomb. The British had retaken the city.

- Capture of Bahadur Shah Zafar and his sons by William Hodson at Humayun's tomb on 20 September 1857

The troops of the besieging force proceeded to loot and pillage the city. A large number of the citizens were killed in retaliation for the British and Indian civilians that had been slaughtered by the rebels. During the street fighting, artillery was set up in the city's main mosque. Neighbourhoods within range were bombarded; the homes of the Muslim nobility that contained innumerable cultural, artistic, literary and monetary riches were destroyed.

The British soon arrested Bahadur Shah Zafar, and the next day the British agent William Hodson had his sons Mirza Mughal, Mirza Khizr Sultan, and grandson Mirza Abu Bakr shot under his own authority at the Khooni Darwaza (the bloody gate) near Delhi Gate. On hearing the news Zafar reacted with shocked silence while his wife Zinat Mahal was content as she believed her son was now Zafar's heir. Shortly after the fall of Delhi, the victorious attackers organised a column that relieved another besieged Company force in Agra, and then pressed on to Cawnpore, which had also recently been retaken. This gave the Company forces a continuous, although still tenuous, line of communication from the east to west of India.

- Cawnpore (Kanpur)

A memorial erected (circa 1860) by the British after the Mutiny at the Bibighar Well. After India's Independence the statue was moved to the All Souls Memorial Church, Cawnpore. Albumen silver print by Samuel Bourne, 1860

In June, sepoys under General Wheeler in Cawnpore (now Kanpur) rebelled and besieged the British entrenchment. Wheeler was not only a veteran and respected soldier but also married to an Indian woman. He had relied on his own prestige, and his cordial relations with the Nana Sahib to thwart rebellion, and took comparatively few measures to prepare fortifications and lay in supplies and ammunition.

The besieged endured three weeks of the Siege of Cawnpore with little water or food, suffering continuous casualties to men, women and children. On 25 June Nana Sahib made an offer of safe passage to Allahabad. With barely three days' food rations remaining, the British agreed provided they could keep their small arms and that the evacuation should take place in daylight on the morning of the 27th (the Nana Sahib wanted the evacuation to take place on the night of the 26th). Early in the morning of 27 June, the British party left their entrenchment and made their way to the river where boats provided by the Nana Sahib were waiting to take them to Allahabad.

Several sepoys who had stayed loyal to the Company were removed by the mutineers and killed, either because of their loyalty or because "they had become Christian". A few injured British officers trailing the column were also apparently hacked to death by angry sepoys. After the British party had largely arrived at the dock, which was surrounded by sepoys positioned on both banks of the Ganges,with clear lines of fire, firing broke out and the boats were abandoned by their crew, and caught or were set on fire using pieces of red hot charcoal. The British party tried to push the boats off but all except three remained stuck. One boat with over a dozen wounded men initially escaped, but later grounded, was caught by mutineers and pushed back down the river towards the carnage at Cawnpore. Towards the end rebel cavalry rode into the water to finish off any survivors.

After the firing ceased the survivors were rounded up and the men shot. By the time the massacre was over, most of the male members of the party were dead while the surviving women and children were removed and held hostage to be later killed in the Bibighar massacre. Only four men eventually escaped alive from Cawnpore on one of the boats: two private soldiers, a lieutenant, and Captain Mowbray Thomson, who wrote a first-hand account of his experiences entitled The Story of Cawnpore (London, 1859).

During his trial, Tatya Tope denied the existence of any such plan and described the incident in the following terms: the British had already boarded the boats and Tatya Tope raised his right hand to signal their departure. That very moment someone from the crowd blew a loud bugle, which created disorder and in the ongoing bewilderment, the boatmen jumped off the boats. The rebels started shooting indiscriminately. Nana Sahib, who was staying in Savada Kothi (Bungalow) nearby, was informed about what was happening and immediately came to stop it. Some British histories allow that it might well have been the result of accident or error; someone accidentally or maliciously fired a shot, the panic-stricken British opened fire, and it became impossible to stop the massacre.

The surviving women and children were taken to the Nana Sahib and then confined first to the Savada Kothi and then to the home of the local magistrate's clerk (the Bibighar) where they were joined by refugees from Fatehgarh. Overall five men and two hundred and six women and children were confined in The Bibigarh for about two weeks. In one week 25 were brought out dead, from dysentery and cholera.

Meanwhile, a Company relief force that had advanced from Allahabad defeated the Indians and by 15 July it was clear that the Nana Sahib would not be able to hold Cawnpore and a decision was made by the Nana Sahib and other leading rebels that the hostages must be killed. After the sepoys refused to carry out this order, two Muslim butchers, two Hindu peasants and one of Nana's bodyguards went into The Bibigarh. Armed with knives and hatchets they murdered the women and children. After the massacre the walls were covered in bloody hand prints, and the floor littered with fragments of human limbs. The dead and the dying were thrown down a nearby well. When the 50-foot (15 m) deep well was filled with remains to within 6 feet (1.8 m) of the top, the remainder were thrown into the Ganges.

Historians have given many reasons for this act of cruelty. With Company forces approaching Cawnpore and some believing that they would not advance if there were no hostages to save, their murders were ordered. Or perhaps it was to ensure that no information was leaked after the fall of Cawnpore. Other historians have suggested that the killings were an attempt to undermine Nana Sahib's relationship with the British. Perhaps it was due to fear, the fear of being recognised by some of the prisoners for having taken part in the earlier firings.

· A contemporary image of the massacre at the Satichaura Ghat

The killing of the women and children hardened British attitudes against the sepoys. The British public was aghast and the anti-Imperial and pro-Indian proponents lost all their support. Cawnpore became a war cry for the British and their allies for the rest of the conflict. Nana Sahib disappeared near the end of the Rebellion and it is not known what happened to him.

Other British accounts state that indiscriminate punitive measures were taken in early June, two weeks before the murders at the Bibighar (but after those at both Meerut and Delhi), specifically by Lieutenant Colonel James George Smith Neill of the Madras Fusiliers, commanding at Allahabad while moving towards Cawnpore. At the nearby town of Fatehpur, a mob had attacked and murdered the local British population. On this pretext, Neill ordered all villages beside the Grand Trunk Road to be burned and their inhabitants to be killed by hanging. Neill's methods were "ruthless and horrible" and far from intimidating the population, may well have induced previously undecided sepoys and communities to revolt.

Neill was killed in action at Lucknow on 26 September and was never called to account for his punitive measures, though contemporary British sources lionised him and his "gallant blue caps". When the British retook Cawnpore, the soldiers took their sepoy prisoners to the Bibighar and forced them to lick the bloodstains from the walls and floor. They then hanged or "blew from the cannon", the traditional Mughal punishment for mutiny, the majority of the sepoy prisoners. Although some claimed the sepoys took no actual part in the killings themselves, they did not act to stop it and this was acknowledged by Captain Thompson after the British departed Cawnpore for a second time.

- Siege of Lucknow

The interior of the Secundra Bagh, several months after its storming during the second relief of Lucknow. Albumen silver print by Felice Beato, 1858

Very soon after the events at Meerut, rebellion erupted in the state of Awadh (also known as Oudh, in modern-day Uttar Pradesh), which had been annexed barely a year before. The British Commissioner resident at Lucknow, Sir Henry Lawrence, had enough time to fortify his position inside the Residency compound. The defenders, including loyal sepoys, numbered some 1700 men. The rebels' assaults were unsuccessful, so they began a barrage of artillery and musket fire into the compound. Lawrence was one of the first casualties. He was succeeded by John Eardley Inglis. The rebels tried to breach the walls with explosives and bypass them via tunnels that led to underground close combat.486 After 90 days of siege, the defenders were reduced to 300 loyal sepoys, 350 British soldiers and 550 non-combatants.

On 25 September, a relief column under the command of Sir Henry Havelock and accompanied by Sir James Outram (who in theory was his superior) fought its way from Cawnpore to Lucknow in a brief campaign, in which the numerically small column defeated rebel forces in a series of increasingly large battles. This became known as 'The First Relief of Lucknow', as this force was not strong enough to break the siege or extricate themselves, and so was forced to join the garrison. In October, another larger army under the new Commander-in-Chief, Sir Colin Campbell, was finally able to relieve the garrison and on 18 November, they evacuated the defended enclave within the city, the women and children leaving first. They then conducted an orderly withdrawal, firstly to Alambagh 4 miles (6.4 km) north where a force of 4,000 were left to construct a fort, then to Cawnpore, where they defeated an attempt by Tantia Tope to recapture the city in the Second Battle of Cawnpore.

In March 1858, Campbell once again advanced on Lucknow with a large army, meeting up with the force at Alambagh, this time seeking to suppress the rebellion in Awadh. He was aided by a large Nepalese contingent advancing from the north under Jung Bahadur Kunwar Rana. General Dhir Shamsher Kunwar Rana, the youngest brother of Jung Bahadur, also led the Nepalese forces in various parts of India including Lucknow, Benares and Patna. Campbell's advance was slow and methodical, with a force under General Outram crossing the river on cask bridges on 4 March to enable them to fire artillery in flank. Campbell drove the large but disorganised rebel army from Lucknow with the final fighting taking place on 21 March.491 There were few casualties to Campbell's own troops, but his cautious movements allowed large numbers of the rebels to disperse into Awadh. Campbell was forced to spend the summer and autumn dealing with scattered pockets of resistance while losing men to heat, disease and guerrilla actions.

· Harayana

In Harayana Rao Tula Ram played a key role in uprising against British. Around 17 May 1857 Rao Tula Ram occupied all government buildings. An army of 5000 was raised to fight the British. Rao Tula Ram was at the point of defeating the British forces when Naga sadhus from Jaipur and Sikh Army from Jind, Kapurthala and Patiala rescued the British forces. On 16 Nov 1857 the combined forces of British, sikhs , Naga sadhus along with artillery support won. Later he joined Tantya Tope, after the defeat of Tantya Tope he left India to meet rulers of Iran, Afghanistan and Russia to keep fighting against the British.

· Jhansi Central India Campaign (1858)

Jhansi Fort, which was taken over by rebel forces, and subsequently defended against British recapture by the Rani of Jhansi

Jhansi State was a Maratha-ruled princely state in Bundelkhand. When the Raja of Jhansi died without a biological male heir in 1853, it was annexed to the British Raj by the Governor-General of India under the doctrine of lapse. His widow Rani Lakshmi Bai, the Rani of Jhansi, protested against the denial of rights of their adopted son. When war broke out, Jhansi quickly became a centre of the rebellion. A small group of Company officials and their families took refuge in Jhansi Fort, and the Rani negotiated their evacuation. However, when they left the fort they were massacred by the rebels over whom the Rani had no control; the British suspected the Rani of complicity, despite her repeated denials.

By the end of June 1857, the Company had lost control of much of Bundelkhand and eastern Rajasthan. The Bengal Army units in the area, having rebelled, marched to take part in the battles for Delhi and Cawnpore. The many princely states that made up this area began warring amongst themselves. In September and October 1857, the Rani led the successful defence of Jhansi against the invading armies of the neighbouring rajas of Datia and Orchha.

On 3 February, Sir Hugh Rose broke the 3-month siege of Saugor. Thousands of local villagers welcomed him as a liberator, freeing them from rebel occupation.

In March 1858, the Central India Field Force, led by Sir Hugh Rose, advanced on and laid siege to Jhansi. The Company forces captured the city, but the Rani fled in disguise.

After being driven from Jhansi and Kalpi, on 1 June 1858 Rani Lakshmi Bai and a group of Maratha rebels captured the fortress city of Gwalior from the Scindia rulers, who were British allies. This might have reinvigorated the rebellion but the Central India Field Force very quickly advanced against the city. The Rani died on 17 June, the second day of the Battle of Gwalior, probably killed by a carbine shot from the 8th King's Royal Irish Hussars according to the account of three independent Indian representatives. The Company forces recaptured Gwalior within the next three days. In descriptions of the scene of her last battle, she was compared to Joan of Arc by some commentators.

· Indore

Colonel Henry Marion Durand, the then-Company resident at Indore, had brushed away any possibility of uprising in Indore. However, on 1 July, sepoys in Holkar's army revolted and opened fire on the cavalry pickets of the Bhopal Contingent (a locally raised force with British officers). When

Colonel Travers rode forward to charge, the Bhopal Cavalry refused to follow. The Bhopal Infantry also refused orders and instead levelled their guns at British sergeants and officers. Since all possibility of mounting an effective deterrent was lost, Durand decided to gather up all the British residents and escape, although 39 British residents of Indore were killed.

- Siege of Arrah

The rebellion in Bihar was mainly concentrated in the Western regions of the state; however, there were also some outbreaks of plundering and looting in Gaya district. One of the central figures was Kunwar Singh, the 80-year-old Rajput Zamindar of Jagdispur, whose estate was in the process of being sequestrated by the Revenue Board, instigated and assumed the leadership of revolt in Bihar. His efforts were supported by his brother Babu Amar Singh and his commander-in-chief Hare Krishna Singh.

On 25 July, mutiny erupted in the garrisons of Danapur. Mutinying sepoys from the 7th, 8th and 40th regiments of Bengal Native Infantry quickly moved towards the city of Arrah and were joined by Kunwar Singh and his men. Mr. Boyle, a British railway engineer in Arrah, had already prepared an outbuilding on his property for defence against such attacks. As the rebels approached Arrah, all British residents took refuge at Mr. Boyle's house. A siege soon ensued – eighteen civilians and 50 loyal sepoys from the Bengal Military Police Battalion under the command of Herwald Wake, the local magistrate, defended the house against artillery and musketry fire from an estimated 2000 to 3000 mutineers and rebels.

On 29 July 400 men were sent out from Danapur to relieve Arrah, but this force was ambushed by the rebels around a mile away from the siege house, severely defeated, and driven back. On 30 July, Major Vincent Eyre, who was going up the river with his troops and guns, reached Buxar and heard about the siege. He immediately disembarked his guns and troops (the 5th Fusiliers) and started marching towards Arrah, disregarding direct orders not to do so.On 2 August, some 6 miles (9.7 km) short of Arrah, the Major was ambushed by the mutineers and rebels. After an intense fight, the 5th Fusiliers charged and stormed the rebel positions successfully. On 3 August, Major Eyre and his men reached the siege house and successfully ended the siege.

After receiving reinforcements, Major Eyre pursued Kunwar Singh to his palace in Jagdispur; however, Singh had left by the time Eyre's forces arrived. Eyre then proceeded to destroy the palace and the homes of Singh's brothers.

In addition to Kunwar Singh's efforts, there were also rebellions carried out by Hussain Baksh Khan, Ghulam Ali Khan and Fateh Singh among others in Gaya, Nawada and Jehanabad districts.

In Lohardaga district of South Bihar (now in Jharkhand), a major rebellion was led by Thakur Vishwanath Shahdeo who was part of the Nagavanshi dynasty. He was motivated by disputes he had with the Christian Kol tribals who had been grabbing his land and were implicitly supported by the British authorities. The rebels in South Bihar asked him to lead them and he readily accepted this offer. He organised a Mukti Vahini (people's army) with the assistance of nearby zamindars including Pandey Ganpat Rai and Nadir Ali Khan.

• Punjab

What was then referred to by the British as the Punjab was a very large administrative division, centred on Lahore. It included not only the present-day Indian and Pakistani Punjabi regions but also the North West Frontier districts bordering Afghanistan.

Much of the region had been the Sikh Empire, ruled by Ranjit Singh until his death in 1839. The kingdom had then fallen into disorder, with court factions and the Khalsa (the Sikh army) contending for power at the Lahore Durbar (court). After two Anglo-Sikh Wars, the entire region was annexed by the East India Company in 1849. In 1857, the region still contained the highest numbers of both British and Indian troops.

The inhabitants of the Punjab were not as sympathetic to the sepoys as they were elsewhere in India, which limited many of the outbreaks in the Punjab to disjointed uprisings by regiments of sepoys isolated from each other. In some garrisons, notably Ferozepore, indecision on the part of the senior British officers allowed the sepoys to rebel, but the sepoys then left the area, mostly heading for Delhi.

At the most important garrison, that of Peshawar close to the Afghan frontier, many comparatively junior officers ignored their nominal commander, General Reed, and took decisive action. They intercepted the sepoys' mail, thus preventing their coordinating an uprising, and formed a force known as the "Punjab Movable Column" to move rapidly to suppress any revolts as they occurred. When it became clear from the intercepted correspondence that some of the sepoys at Peshawar were on the point of open revolt, the four most disaffected Bengal Native regiments were disarmed by the two British infantry regiments in the cantonment, backed by artillery, on 22 May. This decisive act induced many local chieftains to side with the British.

• Marble Lectern in memory of 35 British soldiers in Jhelum

Jhelum in Punjab saw a mutiny of native troops against the British. Here 35 British soldiers of Her Majesty's 24th Regiment of Foot (South Wales Borderers) were killed by mutineers on 7 July 1857. Among the dead was Captain Francis Spring, the eldest son of Colonel William Spring. To commemorate this event St. John's Church Jhelum was built and the names of those 35 British soldiers are carved on a marble lectern present in that church.

The final large-scale military uprising in the Punjab took place on 9 July, when most of a brigade of sepoys at Sialkot rebelled and began to move to Delhi. They were intercepted by John Nicholson with an equal British force as they tried to cross the Ravi River. After fighting steadily but unsuccessfully for several hours, the sepoys tried to fall back across the river but became trapped on an island. Three days later, Nicholson annihilated the 1,100 trapped sepoys in the Battle of Trimmu Ghat.

The British had been recruiting irregular units from Sikh and Pakhtun communities even before the first unrest among the Bengal units, and the numbers of these were greatly increased during the Rebellion, 34,000 fresh levies eventually being raised.

• Lieutenant William Alexander Kerr, 24th Bombay Native Infantry, near Kolapore, July 1857

At one stage, faced with the need to send troops to reinforce the besiegers of Delhi, the Commissioner of the Punjab (Sir John Lawrence) suggested handing the coveted prize of Peshawar to Dost Mohammed Khan of Afghanistan in return for a pledge of friendship. The British Agents in Peshawar and the adjacent districts were horrified. Referring to the massacre of a retreating British army in 1842, Herbert Edwardes wrote, "Dost Mahomed would not be a mortal Afghan ... if he did not assume our day to be gone in India and follow after us as an enemy. British cannot retreat – Kabul would come again." In the event Lord Canning insisted on Peshawar being held, and Dost Mohammed, whose relations with Britain had been equivocal for over 20 years, remained neutral.

In September 1858 Rai Ahmad Khan Kharal, head of the Khurrul tribe, led an insurrection in the Neeli Bar district, between the Sutlej, Ravi and Chenab rivers. The rebels held the jungles of Gogaira and had some initial successes against the British forces in the area, besieging Major Crawford Chamberlain at Chichawatni. A squadron of Punjabi cavalry sent by Sir John Lawrence raised the siege. Ahmed Khan was killed but the insurgents found a new leader in Mahr Bahawal Fatyana, who maintained the uprising for three months until Government forces penetrated the jungle and scattered the rebel tribesmen.

• Bengal and Tripura

In September 1857, sepoys took control of the treasury in Chittagong. The treasury remained under rebel control for several days. Further mutinies on 18 November saw the 2nd, 3rd and 4th companies of the 34th Bengal Infantry Regiment storming the Chittagong Jail and releasing all prisoners. The mutineers were eventually suppressed by the Gurkha regiments. The mutiny also spread to Kolkata and later Dacca, the former Mughal capital of Bengal. Residents in the city's Lalbagh area were kept awake at night by the rebellion. Sepoys joined hands with the common populace in Jalpaiguri to take control of the city's cantonment. In January 1858, many sepoys received shelter from the royal family of the princely state of Hill Tippera.

The interior areas of Bengal proper were already experiencing growing resistance to Company rule due to the Muslim Faraizi movement.

• Gujarat

In central and north Gujarat, the rebellion was sustained by land owner Jagirdars, Talukdars and Thakors with the support of armed communities of Bhil, Koli, Pathans and Arabs, unlike the mutiny by sepoys in north India. Their main opposition of British was due to Inam commission. The Bet Dwarka island, along with Okhamandal region of Kathiawar peninsula which was under Gaekwad of Baroda State, saw a revolt by the Waghers in January 1858 who, by July 1859, controlled that region. In October 1859, a joint offensive by British, Gaekwad and other princely states troops ousted the rebels and recaptured the region.Orissa

During the rebellion, Surendra Sai was one of the many people broken out of Hazaribagh jail by mutineers. In the middle of September Surendra established himself in Sambalpur's old fort. He quickly organised a meeting with the Assistant Commissioner (Captain Leigh), and Leigh agreed to ask the government to cancel his and his brother's imprisonment while Surendra dispersed his followers. This agreement was soon broken, however, when on 31 September escaped the town and make for Khinda, where his brother was located with a 1,400 man force.

The British quickly moved to send two companies from the 40th Madras Native Infantry from Cuttack on 10 October, and after a forced march reached Khinda on 5 November, only to find the place abandoned as the rebels retreated to the jungle. Much of the country of Sambalpur was under the rebels' control, and they maintained a hit and run guerrilla war for quite some time. In December the British made further preparations to crush the uprising in Sambalpur, and it was temporarily transferred from the Chota Nagpur Division into the Orissa Division of the Bengal Presidency. On the 30th a major battle was fought in which Surendra's brother was killed and the mutineers were routed. In January the British achieved minor successes, capturing a few major villages like Kolabira, and in February calm began to be restored. However, Surendra still held out, and the jungle hampered British parties from capturing him. Additionally, any native daring to collaborate with the British were terrorized along with their family. After a new policy that promised amnesty for mutineers, Surendra surrendered in May 1862.

· British Empire

The authorities in British colonies with an Indian population, sepoy or civilian, took measures to secure themselves against copycat uprisings. In the Straits Settlements and Trinidad the annual Hosay processions were banned, riots broke out in penal settlements in Burma and the Settlements, in Penang the loss of a musket provoked a near riot, and security was boosted especially in locations with an Indian convict population.

· Both sides committed atrocities against civilians

In Oudh alone, some estimates put the toll at 150,000 Indians killed during the war, with 100,000 of them being civilians. The capture of Delhi, Allahabad, Kanpur and Lucknow by British forces were followed by general massacres.

Another notable atrocity was carried out by General Neill who massacred thousands of Indian mutineers and Indian civilians suspected of supporting the rebellion.

The rebels' murder of British women, children and wounded soldiers (including sepoys who sided with the British) at Cawnpore, and the subsequent printing of the events in the British papers, left many British soldiers outraged and seeking revenge. Aside from hanging mutineers, the British had some "blown from cannon," (an old Mughal punishment adopted many years before in India), in which sentenced rebels were tied over the mouths of cannons and blown to pieces when the cannons were fired.

A particular act of cruelty on behalf of the British troops at Cawnpore included forcing many Muslim or Hindu rebels to eat pork or beef, as well as licking buildings freshly stained with blood of the dead before subsequent public hangings.

Practices of torture included "searing with hot irons...dipping in wells and rivers till the victim is half suffocated...sequencing the testicles...putting pepper and red chillies in the eyes or introducing them into the private parts of men and women...prevention of sleep...nipping the flesh with pinners...suspension from the branches of a tree...imprisonment in a room used for storing lime..."

British soldiers also committed sexual violence against Indian women as a form of retaliation against the rebellion. As towns and cities were captured from the sepoys, the British soldiers took their revenge on Indian civilians by committing atrocities and rapes against Indian women.

Most of the British press, outraged by the stories of alleged rape committed by the rebels against British women, as well as the killings of British civilians and wounded British soldiers, did not advocate clemency of any kind towards the Indian population. Governor General Canning ordered moderation in dealing with native sensibilities and earned the scornful sobriquet "Clemency Canning" from the press and later parts of the British public.

In terms of sheer numbers, the casualties were much higher on the Indian side. A letter published after the fall of Delhi in the Bombay Telegraph and reproduced in the British press testified to the scale of the

Indian casualties:

All the city's people found within the walls of the city of Delhi when our troops entered were bayoneted on the spot, and the number was considerable, as you may suppose, when I tell you that in some houses forty and fifty people were hiding. These were not mutineers but residents of the city, who trusted to our well-known mild rule for pardon. I am glad to say they were disappointed.

- British soldiers looting Qaisar Bagh, Lucknow, after its recapture (steel engraving, late 1850s)

From the end of 1857, the British had begun to gain ground again. Lucknow was retaken in March 1858. On 8 July 1858, a peace treaty was signed and the rebellion ended. The last rebels were defeated in Gwalior on 20 June 1858. By 1859, rebel leaders Bakht Khan and Nana Sahib had either been slain or had fled.

Edward Vibart, a 19-year-old officer whose parents, younger brothers, and two of his sisters had died in the Cawnpore massacre, recorded his experience:

The orders went out to shoot every soul.... It was literally murder... I have seen many bloody and awful sights lately but such a one as I witnessed yesterday I pray I never see again. The women were all spared but their screams on seeing their husbands and sons butchered, were most painful... Heaven knows I feel no pity, but when some old grey bearded man is brought and shot before your very eyes, hard must be that man's heart I think who can look on with indifference.

- Execution of mutineers by blowing from a gun by the British, 8 September 1857.

Some British troops adopted a policy of "no prisoners". One officer, Thomas Lowe, remembered how on one occasion his unit had taken 76 prisoners – they were just too tired to carry on killing and needed a rest, he recalled. Later, after a quick trial, the prisoners were lined up with a British soldier standing a couple of yards in front of them. On the order "fire", they were all simultaneously shot, "swept... from their earthly existence".

The aftermath of the rebellion has been the focus of new work using Indian sources and population studies. In The Last Mughal, historian

William Dalrymple examines the effects on the Muslim population of Delhi after the city was retaken by the British and finds that intellectual and economic control of the city shifted from Muslim to Hindu hands because the British, at that time, saw an Islamic hand behind the mutiny.Approximately 6,000 of the 40,000 British living in India were killed.

- Reaction in Britain

The scale of the punishments handed out by the British "Army of Retribution" was considered largely appropriate and justified in a Britain shocked by embellished reports of atrocities carried out against British troops and civilians by the rebels. Accounts of the time frequently reach the "hyperbolic register", according to Christopher Herbert, especially in the often-repeated claim that the "Red Year" of 1857 marked "a terrible break" in British experience. Such was the atmosphere – a national "mood of retribution and despair" that led to "almost universal approval" of the measures taken to pacify the revolt.

Incidents of rape allegedly committed by Indian rebels against British women and girls appalled the British public. These atrocities were often used to justify the British reaction to the rebellion. British newspapers printed various eyewitness accounts of the rape of English women and girls. One such account was published by The Times, regarding an incident where 48 English girls as young as 10 had been raped by Indian rebels in Delhi. Karl Marx criticized this story as false propaganda, and pointed out that the story was written by a clergyman in Bangalore, far from the events of the rebellion, with no evidence to support his allegation.

Individual incidents captured the public's interest and were heavily reported by the press. One such incident was that of General Wheeler's daughter Margaret being forced to live as her captor's concubine, though this was reported to the Victorian public as Margaret killing her rapist then herself. Another version of the story suggested that Margaret had been killed after her abductor had argued with his wife over her.

During the aftermath of the rebellion, a series of exhaustive investigations were carried out by British police and intelligence officials into reports that British women prisoners had been "dishonored" at the Bibighar and elsewhere. One such detailed enquiry was at the direction of Lord Canning. The consensus was that there was no convincing evidence of such crimes having been committed, although numbers of British women and children had been killed outright. The term 'Sepoy' or 'Sepoyism' became a derogatory term for nationalists, especially in Ireland.

· Reorganisation

This section needs additional citations for verification. Please help improve this article by adding citations to reliable sources. Unsourced material may be challenged and removed. (May 2017) Bahadur Shah Zafar (the last Mughal emperor) in Delhi, awaiting trial by the British for his role in the Uprising. Photograph by Robert Tytler and Charles Shepherd, May 1858

The proclamation to the "Princes, Chiefs, and People of India," issued by Queen Victoria on 1 November 1858. "We hold ourselves bound to the natives of our Indian territories by the same obligation of duty which bind us to all our other subjects." (p. 2)Bahadur Shah was arrested at Humanyun's tomb and tried for treason by a military commission assembled at Delhi, and exiled to Rangoon where he died in 1862, bringing the Mughal dynasty to an end. In 1877 Queen Victoria took the title of Empress of India on the advice of Prime Minister Benjamin Disraeli.

The rebellion saw the end of the East India Company's rule in India. In August, by the Government of India Act 1858, the company was formally dissolved and its ruling powers over India were transferred to the British Crown. A new British government department, the India Office, was created to handle the governance of India, and its head, the Secretary of State for India, was entrusted with formulating Indian policy. The Governor-General of India gained a new title, Viceroy of India, and implemented the policies devised by the India Office. Some former East India Company territories, such as the Straits Settlements, became colonies in their own right. The British colonial administration embarked on a program of reform, trying to integrate Indian higher castes and rulers into the government and abolishing attempts at Westernization. The Viceroy stopped land grabs, decreed religious tolerance and admitted Indians into civil service, albeit mainly as subordinates.

Essentially the old East India Company bureaucracy remained, though there was a major shift in attitudes. In looking for the causes of the Rebellion the authorities alighted on two things: religion and the economy. On religion it was felt that there had been too much interference with indigenous traditions, both Hindu and Muslim. On the economy it was now believed that the previous attempts by the Company to introduce free market competition had undermined traditional power structures and bonds of loyalty placing the peasantry at the mercy of merchants and money-lenders. In consequence the new British Raj was constructed in part around a conservative agenda, based on a preservation of tradition and hierarchy.

On a political level it was also felt that the previous lack of consultation between rulers and ruled had been another significant factor in contributing to the uprising. In consequence, Indians were drawn into government at a local level. Though this was on a limited scale a crucial precedent had been set, with the creation of a new 'white collar' Indian elite, further stimulated by the opening of universities at Calcutta, Bombay and Madras, a result of the Indian Universities Act. So, alongside the values of traditional and ancient India, a new professional middle class was starting to arise, in no way bound by the values of the past. Their ambition can only have been stimulated by Queen Victoria's Proclamation of November 1858, in which it is expressly stated, "We hold ourselves bound to the natives of our Indian territories by the same obligations of duty which bind us to our other subjects...it is our further will that... our subjects of whatever race or creed, be freely and impartially admitted to offices in our service, the duties of which they may be qualified by their education, ability and integrity, duly to discharge."

Acting on these sentiments, Lord Ripon, viceroy from 1880 to 1885, extended the powers of local self-government and sought to remove racial practices in the law courts by the Ilbert Bill. But a policy at once liberal and progressive at one turn was reactionary and backward at the next, creating new elites and confirming old attitudes. The Ilbert Bill had the effect only of causing a white mutiny and the end of the prospect of perfect equality before the law. In 1886 measures were adopted to restrict Indian entry into the civil service.

• Military reorganisation

Captain C Scott of the Gen. Sir. Hope Grant's Column, Madras Regiment, who fell on the attack of Fort of Kohlee, 1858. Memorial at the St. Mary's Church, Madras

- Memorial inside the York Minster

The Bengal army dominated the Indian army before 1857 and a direct result after the rebellion was the scaling back of the size of the Bengali contingent in the army.The Brahmin presence in the Bengal Army was reduced because of their perceived primary role as mutineers. The British looked for increased recruitment in the Punjab for the Bengal army as a result of the apparent discontent that resulted in the Sepoy conflict.

The rebellion transformed both the native and British armies of British India. Of the 74 regular Bengal Native Infantry regiments in existence at the beginning of 1857, only twelve escaped mutiny or disbandment. All ten of the Bengal Light Cavalry regiments were lost. The old Bengal Army had accordingly almost completely vanished from the order of battle. These troops were replaced by new units recruited from castes hitherto under-utilised by the British and from the minority so-called "Martial Races", such as the Sikhs and the Gurkhas.

The inefficiencies of the old organisation, which had estranged sepoys from their British officers, were addressed, and the post-1857 units were mainly organised on the "irregular" system. From 1797 until the rebellion of 1857, each regular Bengal Native Infantry regiment had had 22 or 23 British officers, who held every position of authority down to the second-in-command of each company. In irregular units there were fewer British officers, but they associated themselves far more closely with their soldiers, while more responsibility was given to the Indian officers.

The British increased the ratio of British to Indian soldiers within India. From 1861 Indian artillery was replaced by British units, except for a few mountain batteries. The post-rebellion changes formed the basis of the military organisation of British India until the early 20th century.

- Historiography Panic of 1857

The Mutiny Memorial in Delhi, a monument to those killed on the British side during the fighting.

Adas (1971) examines the historiography with emphasis on the four major approaches: the Indian nationalist view; the Marxist analysis; the view of the Rebellion as a traditionalist rebellion; and intensive studies of local uprisings. Many of the key primary and secondary sources appear in Biswamoy Pati, ed. 1857 Rebellion.

Suppression of the Indian Revolt by the English, which depicts the execution of mutineers by blowing from a gun by the British, a painting by Vasily Vereshchagin c. 1884. Note: This painting was allegedly bought by the British crown and possibly destroyed (current whereabouts unknown). It anachronistically depicts the events of 1857 with soldiers wearing (then current) uniforms of the late 19th century.

Thomas Metcalf has stressed the importance of the work by Cambridge professor Eric Stokes (1924–1981), especially Stokes' The Peasant and the Raj: Studies in Agrarian Society and Peasant Rebellion in Colonial India (1978). Metcalf says Stokes undermines the assumption that 1857 was a response to general causes emanating from entire classes of people. Instead, Stokes argues that 1) those Indians who suffered the greatest relative deprivation rebelled and that 2) the decisive factor in precipitating a revolt was the presence of prosperous magnates who supported British rule. Stokes also explores issues of economic development, the nature of privileged landholding, the role of moneylenders, the usefulness of classical rent theory, and, especially, the notion of the "rich peasant".

To Kim Wagner, who has conducted the most recent survey of the literature, modern Indian historiography is yet to move beyond responding to the "prejudice" of colonial accounts. Wagner sees no reason why atrocities committed by Indians should be understated or inflated merely because these things "offend our post-colonial sensibilities".

Wagner also stresses the importance of William Dalrymple's The Last Mughal: The Fall of a Dynasty, Delhi 1857. Dalrymple was assisted by Mahmood Farooqui, who translated key Urdu and Shikastah sources and published a selection in Besieged: Voices from Delhi 1857. Dalrymple emphasized the role of religion, and explored in detail the internal divisions and politico-religious discord amongst the rebels. He did not discover much in the way of proto-nationalism or any of the roots of modern India in the rebellion. Sabbaq Ahmed has looked at the ways in which ideologies of royalism, militarism, and Jihad influenced the behaviour of contending Muslim factions.

Almost from the moment the first sepoys mutinied in Meerut, the nature and the scope of the Indian Rebellion of 1857 has been contested and argued over. Speaking in the House of Commons in July 1857, Benjamin Disraeli labelled it a 'national revolt' while Lord Palmerston, the Prime Minister, tried to downplay the scope and the significance of the event as a 'mere military mutiny'. Reflecting this debate, an early historian of the rebellion,

Charles Ball, used the word mutiny in his title, but labelled it a "struggle for liberty and independence as a people" in the text. Historians remain divided on whether the rebellion can properly be considered a war of Indian independence or not, although it is popularly considered to be one in India. Arguments against include:

- A united India did not exist at that time in political, cultural, or ethnic terms

1. The rebellion was put down with the help of other Indian soldiers drawn from the Madras Army, the Bombay Army and the Sikh regiments; 80% of the East India Company forces were Indian
2. Many of the local rulers fought amongst themselves rather than uniting against the British;
3. Many rebel Sepoy regiments disbanded and went home rather than fight;
4. Not all of the rebels accepted the return of the Mughals
5. The King of Delhi had no real control over the mutineers
6. The revolt was largely limited to north and central India. Whilst risings occurred elsewhere they had little impact because of their limited nature;
7. A number of revolts occurred in areas not under British rule, and against native rulers, often as a result of local internal politics;
8. "The revolt was fractured along religious, ethnic and regional lines.
9. The hanging of two participants in the Indian Rebellion, Sepoys of the 31st Native Infantry. Albumen silver print by Felice Beato, 1857.
10. A second school of thought while acknowledging the validity of the above-mentioned arguments opines that this rebellion may indeed be called a war of India's independence. The reasons advanced are:
11. Even though the rebellion had various causes, most of the rebel sepoys who were able to do so, made their way to Delhi to revive the old Mughal empire that signified national unity for even the Hindus amongst them;
12. There was a widespread popular revolt in many areas such as Awadh, Bundelkhand and Rohilkhand. The rebellion was therefore more than just a military rebellion, and it spanned more than one region;
13. The sepoys did not seek to revive small kingdoms in their regions, instead they repeatedly proclaimed a "country-wide rule" of the Mughals and vowed to drive out the British from "India", as they knew it then. (The sepoys ignored local princes and proclaimed in cities they took over: Khalq Khuda Ki, Mulk Badshah Ka, Hukm Subahdar Sipahi Bahadur Ka

– "the people belong to God, the country to the Emperor and authority to the Sepoy Commandant"). The objective of driving out "foreigners" from not only one's own area but from their conception of the entirety of "India", signifies a nationalist sentiment.

Thank You

Thank You For Reading This Book And Shared This Book To Friends As Birthday Gift Have A Wonderfull Day.